One
in Christ™

God's Action Plan

Junior High Student Book

CONCORDIA PUBLISHING HOUSE · SAINT LOUIS

Copyright © 2012 Concordia Publishing House
3558 S. Jefferson Ave., St. Louis, MO 63118-3968
1-800-325-3040 • cph.org

Writers: Kirstin Genthner, Stephenie Hovland, Julaine Kammrath, Sara Knea, Carrie Kober, Mary Lou Krause, Juanita Krueger, Jill Otte, Karla Roeglin, Annette Skibbe, A. Trevor Sutton, Virginia Terrell, Patricia Thies

Editor: Rodney L. Rathmann

Series editors: Rodney L. Rathmann, Carolyn Bergt, Brenda Trunkhill

Editorial assistant: Amanda G. Lansche

Cover art: © CPH/*Creation*, Robert Papp/*Birth of Jesus*, Corbert Gauthier/*Good Friday*, Robert Papp

Manufactured in Shenzhen, China/055760/414111

4   5   6   7   8   9   10   11   12   13   28   27   26   25   24   23   22   21   20   19

Table of Contents

1

CREATION AND FALL

In the Dark

If someone does not have a clue, or if people do not seem to know anything on a subject, then we say they are "in the dark." Conversely, if someone suddenly gets it, sees the truth, or finds an answer, we say "a light comes on." We find many people who are in the dark when it comes to creation, the fall into sin, and God's redemptive plan. Investigate the following false ideas and theories.

Darkness

Evolution—the widely held belief that through "natural selection" organisms became more complex and enhanced. Finally, man evolved from an apelike creature. Although introduced as a theory, many scientists teach evolution as a fact.

BAD NEWS: _____

_____

Sinlessness—belief that we are born innocent. If there is sin, we learn it from others. Or something is wrong only if it hurts someone else. Or, we can make decisions by what feels right or is in line with what society thinks.

BAD NEWS: _____

_____

Earning heaven—belief that if you work hard to do good and are basically a good person, you will go to heaven. Or, as long as you believe in *something*, you will go to heaven after you die.

BAD NEWS: _____

_____

REVIEW

Match each word to the phrase that best describes it.

Redemption

Evolution

Natural Selection

a. theory that states weaker species die out while stronger species evolve into stronger, more complex species

b. theory that states all living things evolved from a single organism

c. deliverance from sin, salvation

In the Light

We have heard the lies Satan puts in our path. We now turn on the light and read God's Word. Shed some light on the false beliefs of the world.

Light

CREATION

1. God created the world in six days. He set the seventh day aside to rest. As you look at the things God created on each day, which day's creation amazes you most? _____

   Why? _____

2. God uses repetition to show how He created everything. How did God create? "And God _____ ." Genesis 1:3, 6, 9, 11, 14, 20, 24, 26. "And it was _____ ." Why is this also important?

   _____

   _____

   _____

   _____

GOOD NEWS: _____

_____

THE FALL

1. Read Genesis 2:15–17. What was the command God gave Adam and Eve?

   _____

   _____

   What would happen if they disobeyed?

   _____

2. Read Genesis 3:1–5. Satan used God as the enemy in his temptation. He convinced Eve that God was holding back something good from her. According to Satan, what would happen if Eve ate of the fruit from the tree of the knowledge of good and evil?

   _____

   _____

GOOD NEWS: _____

_____

REDEMPTION

1. Read Genesis 3:8–13. How did the relationship between man and God change?

   _____

2. Read Genesis 3:14–15. God shows how He is going to defeat sin, death, and Satan in these verses. Who is the offspring that will be in conflict with Satan? _____ What will He do to Satan? _____

3. Read Genesis 3:16–19. What are some of the consequences of the first sin?

   _____

   _____

   _____

4. Read Genesis 3:20–24. God shows His continued care and provision for man after the fall. How did God take care of Adam and Eve after they sinned?

   _____

   _____

   _____

GOOD NEWS:

_____

_____

_____

_____

> **REMEMBER**
>
> The people dwelling in darkness have seen a great light.
>
> Matthew 4:16

2

THE GREAT FLOOD

This Is Serious . . .

Sin. Transgressions. Iniquities. It is some serious business when we do not measure up to God's Law. But if we stop and think about it, sin is often downplayed. Into which category do the following sins fall?

SIN

Who thinks it is wrong?	Almost Everyone	Some People	Almost Nobody
Thoughts, Words, or Actions			

Murder

Abortion

Euthanasia

Taking a few supplies from work

Taking a dollar from a family member

Robbing a bank

Taking illegal substances

Overdrinking

Overeating

Texting OMG

Cursing

Gossiping

Lying

Telling a white lie

Living together before marriage

Homosexuality

Pornography

Gambling

Overspending

Hatred

Pride

Jealousy

Envy

What Does God Think?

Read Genesis 6:1–17. Describe God's attitude toward sin as evidenced in the account of the flood.

REVIEW

Write three synonyms for the word *sin*.

Write one synonym for the word *covenant*.

Some Serious Forgiveness . . .

The Great Flood is not just about sin and its consequences. God shows His incredible grace, mercy, and forgiveness at every turn. Read about the flood in Genesis 6–9. Tell how God showed grace through each of the following:

NOAH   ARK

BOW IN THE   ANIMALS   OLIVE LEAF
CLOUDS

All of the promises of God are complete in the blood of Christ. Write the name of Jesus beneath the cross and rainbow at the upper right.

Are You Serious?

God commands that we take both sin and forgiveness seriously. When it comes to sin, we often want to take the easy way out. Often it seems easier to just go along with a sin. When it comes to forgiveness, we often let pride get in the way. We often find it hard to grant forgiveness. Read the following situations. What would be the easy thing to say or do? What is the response based on God's Word?

1. A friend is telling you some juicy gossip about another friend. It is all very negative and could be very damaging to his reputation.

   You COULD _____. You SHOULD _____
   (Ephesians 4:29).

2. A classmate is bragging that the teacher believed her about the forged permission slip she brought in today.

   You COULD _____. You SHOULD

   _____ (Psalm 101:7).

3. You did not get invited to a friend's party. She has been ignoring you at school. You are hurt and upset. She calls one night to apologize and ask for your help with a project.

   You COULD _____. You SHOULD

   _____ (Colossians 3:12–14).

> **REMEMBER**
>
> By faith Noah, being warned by God concerning events as yet unseen, in reverent fear constructed an ark for the saving of his household.
>
> Hebrews 11:7

3

GOD'S PROMISE TO ABRAM

Moving Day

Read Genesis 12 and 15. Find out what Abram knew before he answered God's call and moved.

God's Call

(Genesis 12:1) Go from

_____,

_____, and

_____.

Go to _____

_____.

God's Promise

(Genesis 12:2) I will _____.

I will _____ and _____.

I will _____

and in you _____.

More promises to Abram: Genesis 15:4 _____

Genesis 15:5 _____

What was Abram's response to God's Word? Genesis 15:6 _____

REVIEW

Use the story of Abram to describe the relationship between these words: *covenant, heir, offspring.*

Where You Belong

Define Abram's family (Galatians 3:7–9):

_____

How do you fit into Abram's family (Galatians 3:27–29)? _____

_____

Personalize the Family Tree. Put yourself, Abram, and others in God's Family Tree.

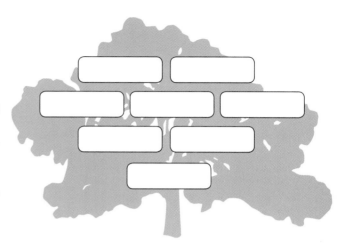

Promises You Can Count On

Check out these promises from God. In the stars, tell how each is important in your life.

Faith: the assurance of things hoped for, the conviction of things not seen. Hebrews 11:1

How did Abram show faith in God?

John 10:27–29

Joshua 1:9

Psalm 50:15

REMEMBER

By faith Abraham obeyed when he was called to go out to a place that he was to receive as an inheritance. And he went out, not knowing where he was going. By faith he went to live in the land of promise, as in a foreign land, living in tents with Isaac and Jacob, heirs with him of the same promise.

Hebrews 11:8–9

THE OFFERING OF ISAAC

A Journey of Faith . . .

How do you decide what to do when you face hard choices?

Read Genesis 21:1–8 and Genesis 22:1–19 to learn how Abraham faced a test.

Write or draw the steps in Abraham's journey.

Genesis 22:11–13

Genesis 22:9–10

Genesis 22:4–8

Genesis 22:3

Genesis 22:2

REVIEW

prototype—

foreshadow—

sacrifice—

only-begotten son—

The Lamb

Use this graphic organizer to view the scriptural inspiration for the hymn "The Lamb." Review Scripture passages on the left. Next, examine the words in the hymn stanzas (see *LSB* 547) and copy into each box on the right those words from the hymn that seem to reflect the meaning of each Scripture verse.

Scriptural Inspiration   Hymn Reflection

"Worthy is the Lamb who was slain, to receive power and wealth and wisdom and might and honor and glory and blessing!" And I heard every creature in heaven and on earth and under the earth and in the sea, and all that is in them, saying, "To Him who sits on the throne and to the Lamb be blessing and honor and glory and might forever and ever!" (Revelation 5:12–13)

And Isaac said to his father Abraham, "My father!" And he said, "Here am I, my son." He said, "Behold, the fire and the wood, but where is the lamb for a burnt offering?" Abraham said, "God will provide for Himself the lamb for a burnt offering, my son." So they went both of them together. (Genesis 22:7–8)

He Himself bore our sins in His body on the tree, that we might die to sin and live to righteousness. By His wounds you have been healed. For you were straying like sheep, but have now returned to the Shepherd and Overseer of your souls. (1 Peter 2:24–25)

Abraham and You . . . Same Family, Same Heritage

Check out Genesis 22:18 and Galatians 3:14, 26–29. Explain the connection.

_____

5

THE CALL OF MOSES

Rescue

Directions: As your teacher directs, write beside each picture what would happen if . . .

God Is Tenacious to Save

Moses had all kinds of excuses for not leading the people out of Egypt.
How did God respond to those excuses?

1st Excuse   Exodus 3:12 _____

_____

2nd Excuse   Exodus 3:16–20 _____

_____

3rd Excuse   Exodus 4:3–9 _____

_____

4th Excuse   Exodus 4:12 _____

_____

5th Excuse   Exodus 4:14–15 _____

_____

REVIEW

Illustrate each word:

tenacious

called

tenacious—persistent, tending
to hold fast, cling

called—to invite or summon
with a view to service

Check In

God is always working and

- [ ] I find myself sometimes aware of His presence.

- [ ] I pretty much focus on my activities, my life.

- [ ] I sometimes sense a tug in my spirit to do something God wants.

- [ ] I sometimes sense a tug in my spirit to act, but I figure someone else will take care of it.

- [ ] I read a Bible verse, and certain phrases sometimes seem to stand out.

- [ ] I don't actually read the Bible much.

- [ ] I hear a song, and it seems to direct me, or I hear a sermon/chapel talk, and something stirs inside.

- [ ] I mostly daydream during church.

- [ ] When I wonder if God wants me to join His work, I ask God to confirm this. I pay attention for anything that God might use to respond to my prayer, like an open door in circumstances or an increased passion for action.

- [ ] I check to be sure my feelings are in line with what I know from the Bible.

- [ ] I stay mostly in my comfort zone because, really, I've got to admit, my life is mostly about me.

THE EXODUS

Follow My Lead

True to His promise, God brought the people of Israel out of Egypt (Exodus 12:50). But they still had a long journey. Review the account of Moses and the people of Israel crossing the Red Sea in Exodus 13:17–14:30. Fill in each footstep below with highlights from Israel's journey. Use the verses to guide your reading.

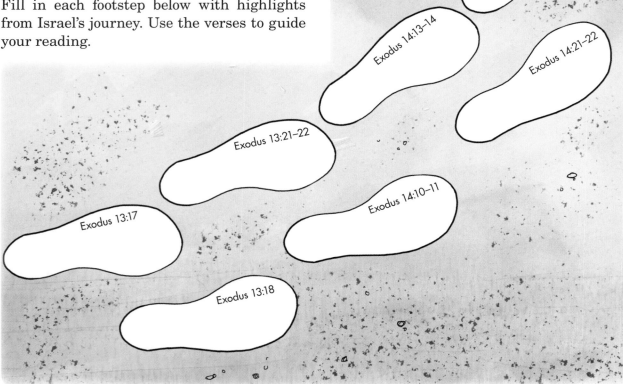

Exodus 14:27–28

Exodus 14:13–14

Exodus 14:21–22

Exodus 13:21–22

Exodus 14:10–11

Exodus 13:17

Exodus 13:18

REVIEW

pillar—

exodus—

Trouble along the Way

Reread the footsteps again. Most show God's great power and love for His people, but one shows sin creeping into the hearts of the people of Israel. Shade in that footstep to remove it from the path.

Even though God's people have witnessed great miracles like the plagues on the Egyptians and are led by a man in direct communication with God, sin still lurks in their hearts. Satan plants the seed of doubt as the people of Israel see Pharaoh's large army coming after them.

Satan works overtime to make us doubt God's power and love. How do the following verses describe Satan's power and human sin?

Be sober-minded; be watchful. Your adversary the devil prowls around like a roaring lion, seeking someone to devour (1 Peter 5:8).

_____

_____

If you do well, will you not be accepted? And if you do not do well, sin is crouching at the door. Its desire is for you, but you must rule over it (Genesis 4:7).

_____

_____

How do you picture Satan using his power?

_____

_____

Satan is sneaky and tricky. He fills us with doubt or fear when we least expect it. In the Bible, there were times when God's "heroes," even Moses himself, sinned and did not see the power of God working in their lives.

The Power of God Is on Our Side

Though we want to trust God fully and follow only Him, God knows that is impossible for us to do on our own. We can try and try, but only Jesus kept the Law perfectly.

How do we benefit from what Christ has done for us (2 Corinthians 5:16–21)?

_____

_____

_____

Read Ephesians 6:11–20. How do we put on the "full armor of God"?

_____

_____

_____

_____

_____

_____

_____

_____

_____

REMEMBER

You have led in Your steadfast love the people whom You have redeemed; You have guided them by Your strength to Your holy abode.

Exodus 15:13

7

THE TEN COMMANDMENTS

A Gift of Good Living

The Commandments were to guide the people of Israel in how they were to live and also as a reminder of what God had done for His people. The Commandments also serve these functions in the lives of God's people today.

Imagine that you are looking at books in the library or bookstore when you discover a shelf labeled The Good Life. Upon closer examination of the titles, you discover that the shelf contains ten books, one for each of the Commandments. Write the number of each of the Ten Commandments in the blank on the spine of the book to which it most closely relates.

REVIEW

honor—

covet—

testimony—

Why We Need God's Law

God's Word teaches that we need God's Law to do three things for us:

Curb	Mirror	Guide

_____

_____

Sin came into the world through Adam, and a consequence of sin is death. Because we were born sinful, we cannot keep God's Commandments and live the good life He intended. The Commandments help to show us our sin. Although we try to keep them, our sinful nature ultimately leads us to disobey.

What Can We Do about Sin?

What do the following verses remind us about our need for a Savior?

Colossians 1:13–14 _____

_____

Romans 10:4 _____

So what can we do about it? Nothing! Christ has done it all for us. We were born sinful, are baptized into the redeeming waters of Baptism, and are made free again. Christ took on the sins of the world and redeemed us.

What does God's Law provide for those who believe in Jesus and are rescued from sin?

Psalm 119:9 _____

_____

REMEMBER

Christ redeemed _____ from the _____ of the _____ by becoming a _____ for us—for it is _____, "Cursed is _____ who is hanged on a tree."

Galatians 3:13

THE SERPENT ON THE POLE

The Serpent and Our Savior

	People in the Wilderness	People Today
Who sinned?	Numbers 21:5 The people	Romans 3:23
What was the consequence of the sin?	Numbers 21:6 The people died	Romans 6:23
What was the plan for saving the people?	Numbers 21:8 Moses made a bronze serpent Put it on a pole People look at it in faith and live	John 3:16
What was lifted up?	Numbers 21:9 Bronze serpent	John 3:14
What needed to happen in order that the people would live?	Numbers 21:9 Look and believe	John 3:15

REVIEW

Draw lines to connect the meanings with three words that describe the life of the Israelites.

rebellion   being led to realize sin and confess it

repentance   turning away from God and His blessings

restoration   being brought back to a trust and belief in God

Look to the Cross

God wants only the best for us. Read John 3:17. For _____ did not _____ His Son into the _____ to _____ the world, but in _____ that the _____ might be _____ through Him.

God rescues those who belong to Him. He forgives our sin for Jesus' sake. He works things for our good.

God used the fiery serpents to call His people back to trusting in Him. God used the death of His Son to reconcile the world to Himself.

How can God work in your life to bring good to you? Discuss the following with your class: how could God bless and grow you as His child as you contend with each?

A bad grade

A sickness or injury

The death of a loved one

An argument with a friend

A rainstorm

A car running out of gas

Running late

Sometimes, God allows us to see the good that comes out of a situation. Other times, it is difficult to see anything good. Of what can we remind ourselves when it is difficult to see the good?

_____

_____

_____

_____

_____

_____

> ### REMEMBER
>
> And as Moses lifted up the serpent in the wilderness, so must the Son of Man be lifted up, that whoever believes in Him may have eternal life.
>
> John 3:14–15

9

RAHAB AND THE SPIES; ISRAEL CROSSES THE JORDAN

Changes for God's People

The Book of Joshua tells the story of many changes.

Moses was dead. Joshua was in charge.

Israel stopped wandering. The people were ready to occupy the Promised Land.

A spy mission went from a previous failure to an exciting success.

After forty years, God stopped the flow of manna. Israel could eat from local crops.

Circumcision was once again practiced, something that had not been practiced regularly during the wandering.

Israel celebrated the Passover.

God caused this good change for His people. The change did not happen without an exciting story. Read that story in Joshua 2. Be ready to explain your answers to these questions:

1. What part of the story did you like best?

2. What part of the story surprised you most?

3. What did you learn about God?

REVIEW

Passover—

manna—

circumcision—

Beginning a New Life

Now it is time to consider the details of the changes. Read Joshua 2:1–14; 2:15–24; 3:14–17; and 5:1–12. Then create a series of newspaper headlines and short articles to summarize the details of each section.

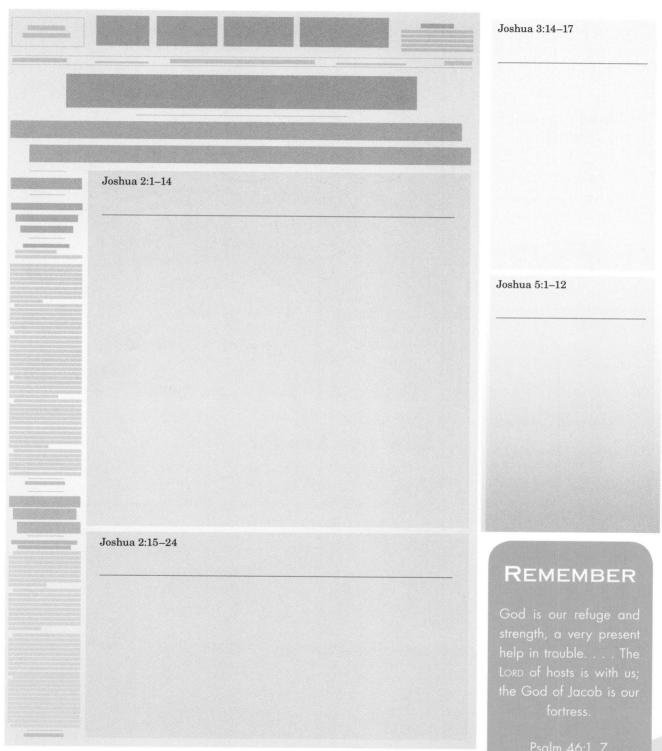

Joshua 3:14–17

Joshua 5:1–12

Joshua 2:1–14

Joshua 2:15–24

REMEMBER

God is our refuge and strength, a very present help in trouble. . . . The LORD of hosts is with us; the God of Jacob is our fortress.

Psalm 46:1, 7

Judges 6–8

GIDEON LEADS GOD'S PEOPLE

What Makes a Good Leader?

What does it take to be a good leader? In the box provided below, think of a great leader in the world today or someone you've learned about in history class. Write his or her name in the bubble provided, and then draw an idea web showing the different qualities that make (or made) that leader great.

Gideon's Leadership Qualities

Now, read Judges 6:11–24, 36–40. As you read, look for the qualities you listed in the activity at the right. Which of them do you see in Gideon? Discuss this with your partner, jot a few notes below, and be prepared to share your ideas with the class.

_____

_____

_____

_____

_____

_____

Leader:

Effective Leaders Are . . .

When you complete the web, share your ideas with the person sitting next to you. Are there any common qualities you both included on your webs? Write those qualities below.

_____

REVIEW

Use your glossary to fill in definitions for the words below.

oppression—

idolatry—

Midianites—

God Gets the Glory

Now read Judges 7:1–8. God makes it very clear through this that the victory will be His victory alone, not Gideon's and not his army's. And if Gideon had any lingering doubts about that, the way God planned the battle must have laid those doubts to rest.

Read Judges 7:15–23, and you'll see just what an awesome battle commander God is.

In the boxes provided, draw a storyboard that shows the sequence of events from the battle. When you're done, share your drawing with the student sitting next to you. Here are some questions you can ask each other:

• What surprises you about the battle plan?

• How do you think Gideon and the other soldiers felt?

• What can we learn about God from this account?

God Gives Us His Strength

God took Gideon, a man who had some serious issues, and gave him the faith and the leadership qualities to conquer a huge army. Over and over again, Gideon doubted his own abilities, and he questioned God and tested Him. He didn't really show any qualities of great leadership at all!

God wants to work through you too. Your life can make an important difference. Take a minute and think about what God might have in store for you. Are there some things you are really good at? some things you really love to do? Maybe God's design for your life features you doing that.

23

11

DAVID BECOMES KING

Why David Waited—God's Purposes Revealed

Scripture indicates that David waited fourteen years from the time Samuel anointed him king of all Israel until the day David finally took the throne. David waited, day by day, month by month. Not only did he wait, but he also waited through some very unpleasant circumstances.

To David, those fourteen years of waiting may, at times, have seemed pointless. Actually, they were quite purposeful. God used them to transform David from a shepherd boy to a godly, wise adult—a leader God's people could confidently follow.

Read each chapter below, looking for the kind of person David had become. What does each incident reveal about the character the Lord had worked in David? How would each characteristic be important to a powerful monarch of God's chosen nation? The first row is done for you.

Scripture	What This Chapter Reveals about David's Character	Why This Characteristic Was Important for Israel's King
2 Samuel 1	David was loyal to Israel's rightful king (Saul) and to his friend, Jonathan. David respected the leader of his nation, obeying the Fourth Commandment.	David modeled respect for authority; this was critical as he himself later worked to unify the kingdom. Assassinations would lead to instability.
2 Samuel 2:1–7		
2 Samuel 4		
2 Samuel 5		
2 Samuel 6		

REVIEW

Define these words, using the glossary as necessary.

type of Christ—

Zion—

ephod—

Faith for Life—Waiting on God

Put yourself in David's sandals or in his sleeping bag on the cold, hard ground. Imagine yourself thinking about Samuel's words and the oil the prophet poured over your head. What questions would be running through your mind? What would you be praying about? List your ideas here:

_____

_____

_____

_____

_____

_____

_____

Talk about these questions with your class:

• Think about your life. For what things are you waiting?

• What makes waiting hard? What's the hardest thing you're waiting for?

• How might Jesus be using this time of waiting to grow or equip you? Where do you already see that happening?

• How might the truths you've encountered today change the ways you're praying (or not praying) for yourself?

REMEMBER

They who wait for the LORD shall renew their strength; they shall mount up with wings like eagles; they shall run and not be weary; they shall walk and not faint.

Isaiah 40:31

25

SOLOMON BUILDS A TEMPLE

The Significance of the Temple

When David was king of Israel, he had the desire to build a place of worship for God's people—one place where they could go to offer sacrifices. God told David, however, that he would not be the one to build the temple. His son, who would be king after him, would build the temple for the Lord. And now the time has come. First Kings 5–8 tells of the preparation and construction of this beautiful house of worship and all that it contained.

Study the drawing of the temple. Note that it consists mostly of two large rooms, one to be used for worship and the other to represent the very presence of God.

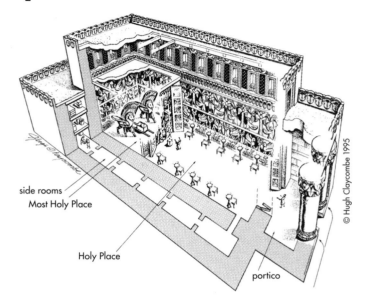

side rooms
Most Holy Place

Holy Place

portico

© Hugh Claycombe 1995

1. Which room is the dwelling place of God? Why do you think so?

2. Which room is used for worship? Why do you think so?

3. Note that a temple curtain separates the two rooms of the temple. A similar curtain tore from top to bottom upon Jesus' death on the cross for the sins of the world (Matthew 27:51). According to the following Bible verse, what does this tearing of the curtain signify?

"We have this as a sure and steadfast anchor of the soul, a hope that enters into the inner place behind the curtain, where Jesus has gone as a forerunner on our behalf, having become a high priest forever after the order of Melchizedek" (Hebrews 6:19–20).

REVIEW

Write the meanings of these words:

Means of Grace—

cherubim—

Under Construction

While we may never be personally involved in the building of such a house of worship, our lives are daily being built into a "spiritual house" as we daily die (confess our sin), receive forgiveness, and rise again to new life by the power of the Holy Spirit. Describe your Christian foundation—what makes you strong in Jesus Christ.

Read the words of 1 Peter 2:5 from the "Remember" section below.

Just as with the construction of any sound building, there is a need to have a solid foundation and building materials.

Check out the Bible verses below and label the cornerstone, the foundation, and the pillars to identify the things described in these verses that support lives being built in Christ.

1 Peter 1:23

Galatians 3:27

Luke 22:19–20

Ephesians 2:20

Ephesians 2:20

REMEMBER

You yourselves like living stones are being built up as a spiritual house, to be a holy priesthood, to offer spiritual sacrifices acceptable to God through Jesus Christ.

1 Peter 2:5

REHOBOAM AND JEROBOAM

Other Gods

God elevated Solomon to the position of king of Israel in place of David, his father. God blessed Solomon with wisdom, wealth, power, and influence. And Solomon posed himself as a key player in the political realm. Note what God's Word says about Solomon's actions and their consequences.

"Now King Solomon loved many foreign women, along with the daughter of Pharaoh: Moabite, Ammonite, Edomite, Sidonian, and Hittite women, from the nations concerning which the LORD had said to the people of Israel, 'You shall not enter into marriage with them, neither shall they with you, for surely they will turn away your heart after their gods.' Solomon clung to these in love. He had 700 wives, princesses, and 300 concubines. And his wives turned away his heart. For when Solomon was old his wives turned away his heart after other gods, and his heart was not

wholly true to the LORD his God, as was the heart of David his father. . . . And the LORD was angry with Solomon, because his heart had turned away from the LORD, the God of Israel, who had appeared to him twice and had commanded him concerning this thing, that he should not go after other gods. But he did not keep what the LORD commanded" (1 Kings 11:1–4, 9–10).

1. Circle the five foreign peoples listed in the above verses with which Solomon aligned himself through marital contracts.

2. In the paragraph above, underline the numbers that indicate Solomon's wives and concubines.

3. Draw a line around the words in the paragraph above that indicate the sad result in Solomon's life.

God Takes Action

1. Read 1 Kings 11:11–13. After the Lord warned Solomon twice about the problems that would come from his idolatry and Solomon refused to listen, God announced His judgment against Solomon. What did God promise to do as a consequence of Solomon's sin?

REVIEW

concubine—

alliance—

remnant—

2. Now skim 1 Kings 11:14–25. Give the names of the two adversaries God raised up against Solomon.

3. Skim 1 Kings 11:26–43. Name the servant to whom God promised to give most of Solomon's kingdom.

God's Word Fulfilled

After King Solomon died, his son Rehoboam became king. No sooner did Rehoboam become king than he faced an important decision. Should he honor the people's request to lighten the workload imposed on them by his father, King Solomon, or should he continue to make them work hard?

He chose to make them work even harder!

This decision caused the people of Israel to revolt against Rehoboam. They then made Jeroboam their king. So now the kingdom of Israel is divided—ten tribes in the Northern Kingdom and two tribes (Judah and Benjamin, commonly regarded as one tribe) in the Southern Kingdom. And so, God's judgment against Solomon because of his sin of idolatry came to pass just as He had said.

Perspectives for Today

Baal and Asherah were among the false gods of Elijah's day. They were crafted from wood and stone, but the wood and stone from which the idols were derived are natural resources—blessings from God also used for many good purposes including the construction of the temple.

Today, there are also elements of creation that draw people's attention away from the one true God. But none of these things is bad in and of itself. These things do not become idols until we allow them to draw our focus away from Jesus, our Savior. Tell how each of the following might be used as either an idol or as a means to give God glory.

money   friends   computers

food   sports   cell phones

Dear heavenly Father, thank You for the gifts that You have given me. You take good care of me and make sure that I have all I need to support this body and life. I have so many other blessings too. Please forgive me for the times that I have put those things in front of You or focused on them instead of Your great love for me. Please show me ways to use those things to bring glory to You and to share Your great love with others.
In Jesus' name. Amen.

REMEMBER

Choose this day whom you will serve. . . . But as for me and my house, we will serve the LORD.

Joshua 24:15

14

2 Kings 23–25;
2 Chronicles 36;
Jeremiah 34–39

GOD'S PEOPLE IN CAPTIVITY

Voices during Troubled Times

Connect the names of the kings and prophet below to the category that describes them better. Were they wicked rebels or faithful servants of God? (Look for their names in these passages: 2 Kings 23–25 and Jeremiah 1. The bold headings in your Bible may help you spot them. Be ready to defend your answers.)

Wicked Rebels

Faithful Servants

Jehoahaz

Josiah

Jehoiakim

Jehoiachin

Jeremiah

Zedekiah

Today's Checkup

Have you ever . . .

_____ forgotten about God's commands?

_____ ignored God's commands?

_____ ignored good advice?

_____ relied on your own goodness to make God happy with you?

_____ thought you were too young to be God's representative?

_____ tried to live a happy life without paying attention to God?

REVIEW

captivity—

rebellious—

faithful—

30

Captive to Sin

Judah sinned and sinned and sinned again. Her sins of idolatry and unbelief were bad enough. But no matter what God's prophets said, Judah's kings ignored His Word. Like their leaders, the people also rejected God's Word and refused to repent. Both leaders and the common people rebelled and refused to obey. Their hearts were as hard as stone!

Finally, God let the Babylonian army defeat His people and rule over them. His goal? To bring His people to repentance and true faith.

What parallels do you see in the lives of God's people today? (Think primarily about your own life!)

WWJD? Why Would Jesus Die?

1. A few years ago, people began using the acronym *WWJD*. It appeared on bracelets, Bible covers, bumper stickers, and in graffiti on walls and railroad cars. It stood for "<u>W</u>hat <u>W</u>ould <u>J</u>esus <u>D</u>o?"

It meant that if you were in a situation and didn't know what to say or how to act, you could make a good decision by asking yourself, "What would Jesus do?" WWJD implied that we should use Jesus as an example of how to behave.

- What is good about that idea?

- What is not so good about it?

2. Jesus' life does model for us what our lives can be like when we trust in Him. It's important to think and pray about being more like Jesus in our words and actions. But before we can do that, before we would *want* to do that, we need to know and believe the answer to the other WWJD question: "<u>W</u>hy <u>W</u>ould <u>J</u>esus <u>D</u>ie?" That question is the difference between eternal life and eternal death. So what's the answer? Why *would* Jesus die?

3. In our culture, leaders (celebrities, politicians, and even some religious people) sometimes suggest that there are many valid ways to find freedom and peace. They say that all religions lead to the same place. They claim that all those paths will get us where we want to go.

How would you answer that claim? What Scripture verses would support your answer?

GOD'S PEOPLE RETURN FROM CAPTIVITY

Where Are You?

Imagine how the emotions of the Jews rose and plunged throughout the times of war with Babylon, the waves of deportation, the process of resettlement in a new land, the Persian takeover of Babylon, the threat of extermination during the reign of King Ahasuerus, and their deliverance from that danger. What a roller coaster! Life for the nation and the individuals in it included a few highs, many terrible lows, and many emotions in between. Only faith in the one true God could have carried His people safely through all this!

We, too, experience a wide array of emotions. The sketches below the graph show different events in the lives of people today. Above each, place a dot on the line that would represent the level of your feelings if you experienced that event. A "1" means you'd be extremely happy, ecstatic with happiness; "10" means you would experience extreme fear or sadness during this event. When you've rated each event, connect the dots from left to right.

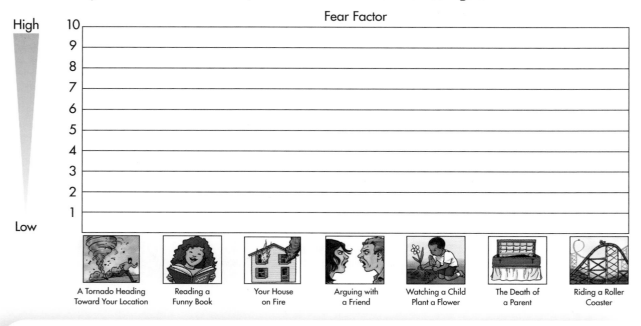

High / Low — Fear Factor

10 9 8 7 6 5 4 3 2 1

A Tornado Heading Toward Your Location | Reading a Funny Book | Your House on Fire | Arguing with a Friend | Watching a Child Plant a Flower | The Death of a Parent | Riding a Roller Coaster

REVIEW

Match these words with their definitions. Use the glossary in the back of this book if you need help. The words come from Ezra 7–8.

vessel   a plea or earnest request

genealogy   a container, like a bottle, bowl, or cup, for holding something

implore   to call or pray for earnestly

entreaty   an account or list of one's ancestors

Who Are They?

The Jews, exiled in Babylon, soon came to appreciate all they had lost. They could no longer worship with other believers in the temple in Jerusalem. The joy of the feasts God had commanded was no longer theirs. Then, one day, they learned that Jerusalem had been destroyed and the temple had been burned. It was a final, terrible blow. But God was not finished with His people. Through Cyrus, the great king of Persia, God would bring His people home and fulfill His promise to send the world's Savior through the descendants of Abraham.

Read Ezra 1–6 and circle *T* for "true" or *F* for "false" by each statement below. Then unscramble the blue letters within the **true** statements and place them on the blanks provided below the True/False activity to reveal a very special name for God.

T / F   1. Those whom God "stirred up" to return to Jerusalem were supported before leaving Persia by their neighbors' gold, silver, and goods.

T / F   2. Nebuchadnezzar kept the temple vessels in a safe place so they could be returned.

T / F   3. The exiles all returned to live in the same town.

T / F   4. Jeshua, his fellow priests, and Zerubbabel built the altar in the temple.

T / F   5. The people built the altar because they feared for their safety.

T / F   6. Everyone shouted cheers of joy when the foundation of the temple was laid.

T / F   7. The leaders allowed the people of the land to assist in building the temple.

T / F   8. Threats by the people of the land made the Jews very fearful; reconstruction was stalled for fifteen years.

T / F   9. Prophecies by Haggai and Zechariah encouraged the people to begin building again.

T / F   10. Darius, king of Persia, made a decree protecting and providing for those who were to rebuild the temple.

What name for God often appears in the Book of Ezra? What makes this name so appropriate?

____ ____ ____   ____ ____ ____   ____ ____

____ ____ ____ ____ ____ ____

Now skip ahead more than fifty years by reading Ezra 7–10. Then talk about the text with your class.

> ### REMEMBER
>
> For I consider that the sufferings of this present time are not worth comparing with the glory that is to be revealed to us.
>
> Romans 8:18

JESUS IS BORN

The Greatest Gift

Last time, we saw that God had revealed His plan of salvation through the promised Messiah in many ways through His prophets. We saw how Jesus fulfilled those prophecies. Today, as you read Luke's account of the nativity (Luke 2:1–20), keep in mind God's plan to save us.

1. The prophet Micah foretold that the Messiah would be born in Bethlehem (Micah 5:2). What did God do to get Mary and Joseph from their hometown of Nazareth to Bethlehem, Joseph's ancestral home, in time for Jesus to be born there?

3. The multitude of angels glorified God as they announced the arrival of the Prince of Peace, the One who would save His people from their sins. According to their words, who will receive God's gift of salvation?

2. Matthew 23:12 says: "Whoever exalts himself will be humbled, and whoever humbles himself will be exalted." How did the birth of Jesus illustrate this concept perfectly?

4. How did the shepherds respond to the message of the angels and to arriving at the birthplace of the infant Jesus?

REVIEW

Draw a line to match each term with its definition.

humility	one of Isaiah's names for Jesus
Prince of Peace	deliverance from sin and its effects
salvation	looking at yourself through God's eyes
incarnation	the act of taking on flesh

True God, True Man

So, baby Jesus was born and laid in a manger in Bethlehem. What makes that the best Christmas gift ever? Jesus was true God and true man at the same time. This made it possible for Him to live a perfect life in our place and then give Himself up as the final sacrifice for the sins of all people. This gift of salvation lasts for all time and is freely offered to every person who ever lived here on earth. It will never break or get lost. It doesn't need batteries. Most important, it's something everyone everywhere truly needs!

Read the following verses and decide whether they tell us that Jesus is true God or true man or both at the same time. Then, write the Bible reference in the appropriate place in the diagram.

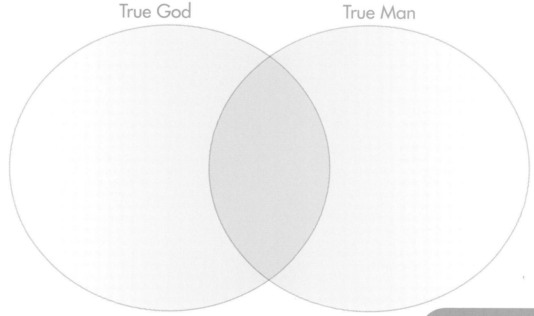

True God   True Man

Matthew 4:2—

Luke 24:39—

John 1:14—

John 19:28—

John 20:28—

Philippians 2:10—

Colossians 2:9—

1 John 5:20—

REMEMBER

For unto _____ is born _____ _____ in the city of David a _____, who is _____ the _____.

Luke 2:11

Jesus became a true human being in order to save us from our sin. As we celebrate the gift of His birth at Christmas, we look ahead to what His incarnation meant. We look ahead to the cross—and to our own salvation. It's the reason He was born in Bethlehem.

JESUS' FIRST DISCIPLES

Fishers of Men

As He began His earthly ministry, Jesus gathered a group of students—the disciples—around Himself. They learned from Jesus and then taught others. They saw Jesus perform miracles and then performed miracles themselves. They watched as Jesus was crucified, and many of them followed Him even into death.

Eventually, Jesus would have hundreds and thousands of disciples. We sometimes take note of the Twelve who were part of our Lord's "inner circle." At first, Jesus called just four individuals—fishermen—to follow Him in "catching" people: Simon, Andrew, James, and John.

At that time, many people made a living by fishing on the Sea of Galilee. These fishermen did not use a rod and reel, worms, or lures to catch one fish at a time.

Instead, much like commercial fishermen today, they used big nets to catch hundreds of fish at a time.

Jesus told Simon and Andrew that He would make them "fishers of men." Rather than spending their days netting fish to feed others' bodies, they would instead now invest their lives in bringing people into the kingdom of God.

Even after the Twelve had spent several years hearing Jesus teach and watching Him minister, they still sometimes misunderstood His methods and priorities. Then Jesus had to correct them. Other times, they knew exactly what He wanted, and Jesus praised them for their work.

Find the following passages and write the letter beside each in the correct column.

a. Matthew 16:13–17   d. Luke 18:34

b. Matthew 16:21–23   e. John 21:4–7

c. Luke 18:15–17   f. Acts 2:37–38

Understanding Their Calling	Misunderstanding Their Calling

REVIEW

Circle the correct meaning of each word below.

A **disciple** is (a) a student who learns from a master/teacher; (b) one of Jesus' inner circle of twelve followers; (c) one of hundreds who followed Jesus during and after His earthly ministry; (d) anyone today who follows Jesus.

A **fisher of men** is (a) someone who works in the sporting goods department; (b) someone who has a job in the church, like a pastor or teacher in a Christian school; (c) someone like me who knows Jesus' love and wants others to know it too; (d) two of the above.

Now Is the Time!

When Jesus called His first disciples, He expected them to follow Him immediately. He expects the same from us. But we don't always drop what we are doing to obey Him. Suppose the Lord walked into your classroom right now or into your gym during practice after school. Would you leave your books or your basketball behind to go with Him? What if He told you to stay where you are, doing your best, and living out His love in your relationships with others? Would worries or fears keep you from doing what He asked?

Sadly, words like *immediately*, *now*, and *instantly* do not always describe our life as Christ's disciples. Jesus forgives our slowness of heart to believe and the reluctance of our feet and hands to act. Though we sometimes misunderstand His calling in our lives, He continues to patiently explain and wait for us.

Though we often struggle with temptation and often disobey, in His cross we find forgiveness for our every failure to live as His disciples.

Talk about each of these questions with one or two other people. Be prepared to report to the class.

1. In Scripture, Jesus commands His disciples to follow Him. What does that mean specifically for you personally and for your classmates right this minute?

2. What fears or concerns keep Christians today from following Jesus? What keeps you from following Him immediately and completely?

3. How does the message Christ proclaimed help you in times like that?

Fishers of Men? Me?

Jesus did not leave His disciples on their own to figure out what He meant when He told them to be "fishers of men." He taught them all about it—lovingly and patiently. He gave them everything they needed—knowledge, skills, practice, His own example to follow. On top of all that, He gave them the Holy Spirit to empower them after He went back to heaven.

The Holy Spirit is at work in our lives too. As He works in us, we sometimes do a great job of following Jesus, leaving our fears and doubts behind. At other times, we do not do as well. We delay, deny, and disobey. At those times especially, we look back to Christ's sacrifice on the cross—His sacrifice for us!

On the line below, put an X on the continuum to show where you think you are as you consider your words and actions as Jesus' disciple and witness. Then, beneath the box on the left, jot down the biggest hindrance to your discipleship. Beneath the box on the right, jot down two or three things that help you most as you grow in your life of discipleship and witness.

Totally Hopeless Fisher of Men	Productive, Successful Fisher of Men

REMEMBER

Jesus said to them again, "Peace be with you. As the Father has sent Me, even so I am sending you." And when He had said this, He breathed on them and said to them, "Receive the Holy Spirit."

John 20:21–22

NICODEMUS VISITS JESUS

Good and Evil—the Ultimate Conflict

God is holy. Man is sinful. From the day Adam and Eve fell into sin, life on earth has been marked by the struggle between good and evil. One human philosophy—dualism—proposes that neither will ever win; life in our universe will remain locked in an ongoing battle forever.

Scripture, though, teaches that Jesus has already won the battle between good and evil on His cross and in His empty tomb. Meanwhile, while we live here on earth, we fight a mop-up operation. When Jesus returns, we will sing, "The kingdom of the world has become the kingdom of our Lord and of His Christ, and He shall reign forever and ever" (Revelation 11:15). Until then, we endure situations that are often scary and dark.

The battle between good and evil, particularly between God and demons, marked Jesus' earthly ministry. Our Savior often confronted Satan head-on—not just during His temptation in the desert, but also when He healed people tormented by devils.

Jesus' conversation with Nicodemus helps us understand these confrontations and what's at stake. Read John 3:1–21. As you do, you will note several opposites. Unscramble the words in column 1 and their opposites in column 3. Then write the contrast in column 4. Use the hints from John 3 (column 5) if you need help. The first one is done for you.

GTHIL	and	KDRA	LIGHT and DARK	John 3:19
TEAH	and	VEOL		—
NEEVAH	and	LELH		John 3:16
FIEL	and	TEHAD		John 3:14–15
DAVES	and	MEDDENONC		John 3:17
AYD	and	THIGN		John 3:2
REALTHY things	and	LYEVANEH things		John 3:12
DEANCS	and	SNECDDE		John 3:13

The Bible tells us every person on earth is on one side or the other. There is no middle ground. Why do people sometimes like to "hang out" on the wrong side? When have you chosen that side? Why?

REVIEW

Conversion is . . .

Conversion is not . . .

Who Was Nicodemus?

Look back over John 3:1–21. Find all the facts about Nicodemus you can glean from this text. Who was he? What did he believe about God and about light and dark, good and evil? What sparked his interest in Jesus?

-
-
-
-
-

Born Again!

Talk about the questions below with your class. As you do so, think about Nicodemus being "born again." What does that phrase mean?

1. Why did Nicodemus come to Jesus? What did he hope Jesus could tell him?

2. How did Jesus answer this?

3. What made Jesus' answer hard for Nicodemus to understand?

4. What can you deduce from Jesus' words in this text about why evil persists in our world?

5. What has God done to address this problem?

6. If God did this, why isn't everyone on the side of the light? Why isn't everyone saved?

REMEMBER

For God so loved the world, that He gave His only Son, that whoever believes in Him should not perish but have eternal life. For God did not send His Son into the world to condemn the world, but in order that the world might be saved through Him.

John 3:16–17

God So Loved _____

Put your name on the blank line above. Sometimes, it's easier for us to think of God loving "the world" than it is to believe that He loves each one of us—deeply and personally.

When is it hard for you to trust God's love for you personally? How can your Baptism help you then?

JESUS HEALS AT BETHESDA

The Pool of Bethesda

Jesus traveled from Galilee to Jerusalem to observe one of the feasts of the Jews. While He was there, Jesus went to the pool called Bethesda (John 5:2), which is near the Sheep Gate, one of the entrances to the temple. Study John 5:3–4; look at your Bible's notes for help. For what was this pool known?

As the text continues, we find that true healing does not come when the sick try to go to the pool. True healing comes when Jesus comes to the sick.

Two Types of Disabilities

In John 5, two groups of people are introduced: the Physically Disabled and the Spiritually Disabled. In the left-hand circle, write some of the characteristics of the physically disabled group described in verses 1–9. In the right-hand circle, write some characteristics of the spiritually disabled group described in verses 10–18.

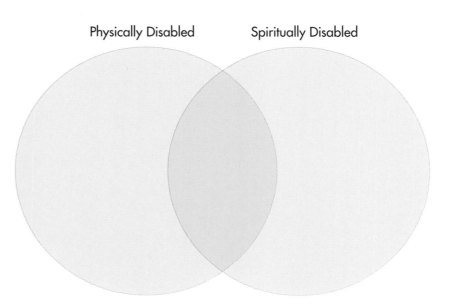

Physically Disabled   Spiritually Disabled

Which group's sickness is ultimately more detrimental to them?

REVIEW

righteousness—

self-righteousness—

Earthly Cure vs. Eternal Cure

God has blessed us with many advancements in technology and medical know-how to improve the quality of life for persons with disabilities or sicknesses. Still, God does not provide earthly healing for everyone. Take the apostle Paul, for example. In 2 Corinthians 12:7–9, Paul writes about an unnamed physical condition: "So to keep me from becoming conceited because of the surpassing greatness of the revelations, a thorn was given me in the flesh, a messenger of Satan to harass me, to keep me from becoming conceited. Three times I pleaded with the Lord about this, that it should leave me. But He said to me, 'My grace is sufficient for you, for My power is made perfect in weakness.' Therefore I will boast all the more gladly of my weaknesses, so that the power of Christ may rest upon me."

Explain Paul's words.

What is the only cure for spiritual sickness and disability?
Read Acts 4:12 and Ephesians 2:8–9.

> ### REMEMBER
>
> For by grace you have been saved through faith. And this is not your own doing; it is the gift of God, not a result of works, so that no one may boast.
>
> Ephesians 2:8–9

PARABLES OF THE KINGDOM

Jesus, the Teacher

As Jesus traveled, He encountered many types of people: some who doubted or refused to believe in Him and others who possessed a strong faith and were committed to following Him to the end. Jesus addressed all types of hearers. Because Jesus is a teacher, He used words and actions to weave pictures of what was happening in the present and what will happen in the near and distant future.

What the Kingdom of Heaven Is Like

In Matthew 13:24–52, Jesus uses parables to teach simple yet profound truths about human existence. He teaches about the Church—the sum of those who by faith know and believe in Him as the Son of God and Savior of the world—and also about those outside the Church—those without faith in Him. Read these verses. Then consider the three Venn diagrams that follow. Each diagram compares two of Jesus' parables about the kingdom of heaven. Fill in blanks to name the parable identified by each set of verses. Then draw lines to place each phrase in the correct area of each Venn diagram.

Parable of the _____

(Matthew 13:24–30, 36–43)

Parable of the _____

(Matthew 13:47–50)

Angels will sort one kind from another.

Angels will burn that which is undesirable.

Every kind of fish is gathered.

Enemy sows bad seed among the good.

Men draw the full net ashore and sort fish.

Good and bad are together until the end.

Master tells the servant to let the good and bad plants grow beside each other.

REVIEW

leaven—

harvest—

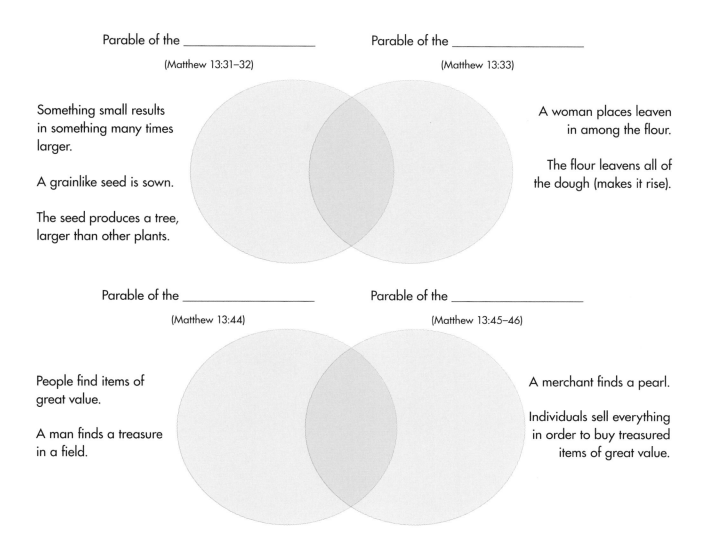

Parable of the _____
(Matthew 13:31–32)

Parable of the _____
(Matthew 13:33)

Something small results in something many times larger.

A grainlike seed is sown.

The seed produces a tree, larger than other plants.

A woman places leaven in among the flour.

The flour leavens all of the dough (makes it rise).

Parable of the _____
(Matthew 13:44)

Parable of the _____
(Matthew 13:45–46)

People find items of great value.

A man finds a treasure in a field.

A merchant finds a pearl.

Individuals sell everything in order to buy treasured items of great value.

A Matter of Cost and Value

To the elderly woman, the sword was just another item cluttering up her attic. She took it to the rummage sale along with other items she found there. She delighted in her clean attic, glad to be rid of years of dust-covered trunks, boxes, and other items long disposed of there.

Michael had been saving every bit of money he received for Christmas and birthday presents and everything he earned working for the neighbors running errands and doing small jobs for them. He intended to buy a game when he accumulated enough money. But when he saw the sword at the rummage sale, he gathered all of his money and even borrowed some from his dad to buy it. The sword was totally cool, and he was going to have it to hang on the wall of his room no matter what.

Jesus died to earn forgiveness and eternal life for all people. Jesus gave His all to save us; it cost Him His life. To some, Jesus' sacrifice means nothing; to those who believe in Him as their Savior, it means everything!

REMEMBER

The Lord will rescue me from every evil deed and bring me safely into His heavenly kingdom. To Him be the glory forever and ever. Amen.

2 Timothy 4:18

JESUS AND THE MIRACULOUS CATCH OF FISH

A Lesson and a Miracle

In today's Bible story, Jesus gathered His first disciples, and He did it by giving them a fishing lesson. Peter and the others did what Jesus told them without hesitation. Jesus worked a miracle for them, and He taught them about much more than how to catch a heavy load of fish.

Read the story for yourself in Luke 5:1–11, and, as you read, take notes on what happens, filling in main events in the appropriate boxes below.

The Lesson	The Miracle	The Decision

REVIEW

Lake of Gennesaret—

disciple—

miracle—

How to Catch People

After Jesus worked His miracle, He spoke using a metaphor to tell Peter, Andrew, James, and John that they were to leave their nets behind and become fishers of men. In both the Old and New Testaments, God calls us to spread the Gospel message to those who are lost. When Jesus told Peter and the others that they would be fishers of men, He was making a comparison to the life's-work kind of fishing rather than the hobby kind.

The day he met Jesus was a life-changing day for Peter. He found a new calling as one of Jesus' disciples. Jesus has called us as well. Read Luke 5:1–11 again. Using the diagram below, work with a partner to fill in the actions Peter took as Jesus transformed him from a fisherman to a fisher of people.

THE GOOD SAMARITAN

Acting It Out

Speaking part: NARRATOR

Actors: TRAVELER, ROBBER(S), PRIEST, LEVITE, SAMARITAN, INNKEEPER

Setting up the scene: ROBBERS should be hiding along a "road." TRAVELER should be prepared to walk along the road.

NARRATOR: A man was going down from Jerusalem to Jericho, (*TRAVELER walks along a "road."*)

NARRATOR: and he fell among robbers, (*ROBBERS leap from hiding place and assault TRAVELER.*)

NARRATOR: who stripped him and beat him (*ROBBERS pantomime beating TRAVELER.*)

NARRATOR: and departed, leaving him half dead. (*ROBBERS EXIT and TRAVELER lies on the floor.*)

NARRATOR: Now by chance a priest was going down that road, (*PRIEST starts walking down the road.*)

NARRATOR: and when he saw him he passed by on the other side. (*PRIEST sees TRAVELER and, in fear and disgust, crosses to the other side of the road, totally ignoring TRAVELER, then EXITS.*)

NARRATOR: So likewise a Levite, when he came to the place and saw him, (*LEVITE starts walking down the road.*)

NARRATOR: passed by on the other side. (*LEVITE, in fear and disgust, crosses to the other side of road, totally ignoring TRAVELER, then EXITS.*)

NARRATOR: But a Samaritan, as he journeyed, came to where he was, (*SAMARITAN starts walking down the path and notices TRAVELER.*)

NARRATOR: and when he saw him, he had compassion. (*SAMARITAN puts hands to face.*)

NARRATOR: He went to him and bound up his wounds, pouring on oil and wine. (*SAMARITAN crosses to TRAVELER, kneels, and pantomimes pouring liquid on his wounds.*)

NARRATOR: Then he set him on his own animal (*SAMARITAN lifts TRAVELER and helps him walk down road.*)

NARRATOR: and brought him to an inn and took care of him. (*SAMARITAN and TRAVELER meet INNKEEPER.*)

NARRATOR: And the next day he took out two denarii and gave them to the innkeeper, (*SAMARITAN pantomimes handing coins to INNKEEPER.*)

NARRATOR: saying, "Take care of him, and whatever more you spend, I will repay you when I come back." (*SAMARITAN walks away from INNKEEPER and sets out on the road again.*)

REVIEW

priest—

Levite—

Samaritan—

The Way of Blood

After you've performed the story of the Good Samaritan, fill in the diagram below. How did each of the following treat the traveler? What did they do to or for him?

Robbers	Priest and Levite	Good Samaritan

Three Lessons

When He had finished telling the story of the Good Samaritan, Jesus asked the lawyer which of the three men was a neighbor, and the lawyer gave the correct answer: the one who showed mercy. Jesus replied, "Go and do likewise." Showing mercy—that sounds easy enough, right? But how easy is it to be merciful and compassionate all the time? Have you always done the compassionate thing? Do you always help those in need? Probably not. None of us do. We're all sinners, and none of us are perfect all the time.

There are three lessons we can learn from the parable of the Good Samaritan:

1. Demonstrating love to others, despite prejudice or hesitation, is not an option.
2. Neighbors can be anyone or everyone.
3. We can't possibly keep the Commandments all the time; therefore, we need a Savior.

Read Romans 3:19–20. What do these verses tell us about our ability to follow the Law? Then read Romans 5:6–8. What comfort can we find here?

Now that you know what God has done for you, how can you be a Good Samaritan?

Something to think about: Were there any times when you were like the injured man? Who came to your rescue?

> ### REMEMBER
>
> By this we know love, that He laid down His life for us, and we ought to lay down our lives for our brothers. But if anyone has the world's goods and sees his brother in need, yet closes his heart against him, how does God's love abide in him? Little children, let us not love in word or talk but in deed and in truth.
>
> 1 John 3:16–18

THE LOST SON

The Loving Parent

Today's Bible story tells us of a young man who received unconditional love. Read Luke 11:15–32, the parable of the lost son. Then number the events of the story below to place them in proper sequence. Finally, write the large letters from items 1 to 17, in order in the spaces below to reveal an important Bible truth.

_____ The youn**g**er son wants his share of the father's property now.

_____ The older bro**t**her becomes angry and refuses to go to the party.

_____ The father runs and **g**reets his lost son with a hug and kiss.

_____ Drough**t** occurs.

_____ The younger son le**a**ves home.

_____ The older brother hears a party from **a** distance.

_____ The fathe**r** divides his property among his sons.

_____ The younger son begins to be in n**e**ed.

_____ The younger son **h**ires out to work feeding pigs.

_____ The younger son goes to a far **C**ountry and squanders his father's money.

_____ The younge**r** son is starving and wants pigs' food.

_____ The yo**U**nger son goes home.

_____ The older brother f**i**nds out about the party in honor of the younger brother.

_____ The younger s**O**n comes to his senses and decides to return home.

_____ The father organizes a party in honor o**f** his son's return.

_____ The younger son repents of his sin to **h**is father.

_____ The father talks with the older brot**h**er and tells him why he is rejoicing.

We are saved by ____ ____ ____ ____ ____

____ ____ ____ ____ ____ ____ ____ ____   ____ ____ ____ ____ ____!

REVIEW

squandered—

compassion—

Welcome Home!

God sent His Son, Jesus, to pay the penalty of sin in our place. Jesus loves us unconditionally. He has forgiven our sins and removed them "as far as the east is from the west" (Psalm 103:12); His love for us is steadfast and unchangeable! Think about your life with Jesus in light of this parable. Match each of the following statements from the story with the connecting application on the right.

_____ 1. The younger son misuses what his father has given him.

_____ 2. The younger son reaches a hopeless state, but then remembers his father.

_____ 3. The younger son plans to return to his father and appeal to him for mercy.

_____ 4. The father welcomes the younger son back unconditionally.

_____ 5. The father celebrates his son's return and honors him.

_____ 6. The older brother resents the treatment of the wayward son.

_____ 7. The younger son was dead and is alive again; he was lost and is found.

a. On our own, we are dead in trespasses and sin; lost eternally.

b. We take God's goodness for granted and follow our own wayward desires.

c. We sometimes criticize God's love and forgiveness for other sinners, telling ourselves we are somehow better than they are.

d. When we are brought to a realization of our unworthiness and sin, God brings us to a remembrance of His love and grace.

e. God welcomes forgiven sinners back into His family, forgiving us for Jesus' sake.

f. With restoration and forgiveness, there is joy and celebration.

g. Realizing our sins, we ask God to forgive us for Jesus' sake.

REMEMBER

See what kind of love the Father has given to us, that we should be called children of God; and so we are.

1 John 3:1

THE LAST SUPPER

Securing the Scene!

Celebrating the Feast of the Unleavened Bread would be somewhat more challenging for the disciples this year! Read Matthew 26:17–30. Jesus and His disciples appeared to be somewhat on the run; they had no permanent dwelling; the Pharisees and most everyone else were watching them for any false moves; not many trusted or respected Jesus. Very soon, Jesus would suffer and die for the sins of the world.

But against this backdrop, Jesus had a very clear plan for the disciples that would enable them to keep the Passover. Write *True* next to the statements in the right-hand column that are true; correct each false statement to make it true.

1. Jesus told them to go and speak with a woman for a room.

   _____

2. The disciples were told what to say.

   _____

3. Jesus told them to call Him Son of God when asking for the room.

   _____

4. The disciples quoted Jesus saying, "My time is at hand."

   _____

5. The disciples did as directed.

   _____

6. Jesus prepared for the Passover.

   _____

7. In this room, Jesus instituted the Lord's Supper.

   _____

REVIEW

unleavened bread—

Passover—

betray—

covenant—

Is It I, Lord?

Once in the room, Jesus reveals the fact that someone will betray Him. One by one, the disciples all asked, "Is it I, Lord?"

Write the name of the betrayer in the circle on the left; write your name in the circle on the right.

Then, look up the Bible passage written where the circles intersect.

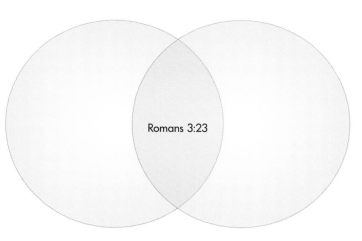

Romans 3:23

What do you, the betrayer, and all other people have in common?

_____

Read 2 Corinthians 5:15 and determine yet another common theme that is communicated.

_____

For the Forgiveness of Sins

Read 1 Corinthians 10:16–17. What does this passage say we receive in Holy Communion?

_____

_____

Draw arrows to show the relationship between Jesus' body and blood with the bread and the wine.

How do worthy recipients receive Holy Communion (2 Corinthians 13:5)?

_____

Christ's body and blood, in, with, and under the bread and the wine convey the forgiveness of sins for those who take Holy Communion in all sincerity and with the knowledge of its benefits. Are we sometimes puzzled by how both the body and bread are present and how both the blood and wine are present? Yes. In spite of being puzzled, however, we can rest secure, knowing that God handles the "how" and works faith in our hearts to believe the "what" and, even more important, the "who" of this life-changing Sacrament! It's all God! He created us, His Son redeemed us, and His Holy Spirit sanctifies us!

JESUS DIES AND IS BURIED

Time to Speak Up

The time has come! The words of God spoken in Genesis 3:15 to the serpent are about to be completed—"I will put enmity between you and the woman, and between your offspring and her offspring; He shall bruise your head, and you shall bruise His heel."

Satan is rejoicing over the "bruising" of Jesus' heel. All things seem to be going in Satan's favor. However, we know the rest of the story. Jesus will not be silent as He "crushes" Satan's head.

Jesus' Words

Jesus crushes Satan's head when He pays for the sins of the world by dying on a cruel wooden cross and then showing His victory by rising from the dead. Jesus spoke seven times while on the cross. Fill in the blanks below to complete three statements about the things Jesus said. Use the following three sets of words:

> the extent of His suffering in our place
>
> the completion of His work to save us
>
> His love and concern for others

With the following words, Jesus shows

_____

"Father, forgive them, for they know not what they do." (Luke 23:34)

"Truly, I say to you, today you will be with Me in Paradise." (Luke 23:43)

"Woman, behold, your son!" "Behold, your mother!" (John 19:26–27)

With the following words, Jesus shows

_____

"My God, My God, why have You forsaken Me?" (Matthew 27:46/Mark 15:34)

"I thirst." (John 19:28)

With the following words, Jesus shows

_____

"It is finished." (John 19:30)

"Father, into Your hands I commit My spirit!" (Luke 23:46)

REVIEW

Match the following words with their definitions

_____ enmity   a. feelings of hatred and hostility

_____ righteousness   b. bought back; recovered ownership of

_____ redeemed   c. the state of being right, holy, and pure

The Centurion's Words

Read Matthew 27:51–52. Fill in the blanks below to indicate amazing things that happened at the death of Christ.

And behold, the _____ . And

_____ , and the _____ . The _____ .

And _____ .

Read Matthew 27:54. What is amazing about the fact that the centurion recognized Jesus as the Son of God, but the high priest and temple leaders did not?

_____

_____

_____

_____

_____

My Words . . . My Actions

Those at the foot of the cross on Good Friday probably wondered what the crucifixion of Jesus meant. They did not understand it at the time, but Jesus' sacrifice guaranteed their eternal life in heaven. We have the blessing of living after the cross and the joyful story of the Easter resurrection.

What words and actions in your life show that you know the enormity of Christ's gift on the cross—what it cost Him and what it gives to you?

_____

_____

_____

_____

_____

_____

_____

REMEMBER

Surely He has borne our griefs and carried our sorrows; yet we esteemed Him stricken, smitten by God, and afflicted. But He was wounded for our transgressions; He was crushed for our iniquities; upon Him was the chastisement that brought us peace, and with His stripes we are healed.

Isaiah 53:4–5

JESUS RISES FROM THE DEAD

Easter at the Empty Tomb

Every one of the Gospels tells the story of the resurrection, which is the most significant event in human history. We're going to focus on Matthew's Gospel. In your group, read Matthew 28:1–15 and answer the questions below.

1. Mary Magdalene and the other Mary go to the tomb at dawn after the Sabbath. Why might they choose this time to go?

2. What do they see as soon as they reach the tomb?

3. Why are the guards "like dead men"? Does their reaction surprise you? Explain.

4. The angel tells the women: "Do not be afraid." Where else have we heard an angel say these words?

5. How do the women feel as they leave the tomb? Why might they feel this way?

6. What do both the angel and Jesus tell the women to do?

7. What do the chief priests tell the guards to say? Why do you think they make up this story?

REVIEW

resurrection—

Sabbath—

Why Easter Matters

Why do you think Easter is the most important day of the year for Christians? The Bible has a lot to say about the powerful meaning of Christ's resurrection. Read the following passages and answer the questions.

	Easter matters because . . .
Romans 1:4	
Hebrews 2:14–15	
1 Corinthians 15:55–57	
Romans 5:15	
Romans 10:9	

Go back to your answer to the question at the beginning of this section.
Do you have anything to add to it?

Easter for the World

In Matthew 28:7 and then again in verse 10, the women who first witnessed the resurrection were told to "Go and tell." The angel told them, and then Jesus told them. The women were told to go quickly, and although they went with fear and trembling, the Bible tells us they ran. How then can we do any differently? The last words Jesus spoke before He ascended are words encouraging His disciples—and us as well—to share the Good News.

Easter is not a message we should hide. It is not a gift we should be ashamed of. It is the most glorious day in the history of the world, and we must share it with others.

In the space below, write a prayer expressing what you've learned in the lesson today about Easter and its importance on the day Christ rose from the dead as well as its importance in our lives.

REMEMBER

For Christ also suffered once for sins, the righteous for the unrighteous, that He might bring us to God, being put to death in the flesh but made alive in the spirit.

1 Peter 3:18

THE ASCENSION

He Came Down; He Ascended

Jesus came to earth for specific reasons. Write the reasons you find recorded in Titus 2:11–14.

_____
_____
_____
_____
_____
_____
_____
_____
_____
_____
_____

Just because Jesus ascended and is gone from sight doesn't mean He abandoned you. When Jesus went to sit at the right hand of His heavenly Father, He sent us the Helper, the Holy Spirit. What is the Helper's job? Read John 16:13.

_____
_____
_____
_____
_____
_____
_____
_____
_____
_____

REVIEW

sanctification—

Gazing Upward

Read Acts 1:1–11. Then record the basic facts from the story as appropriate in each frame below.

Commands	Promises	Questions

Answers Given	Actions

What's Next?

Just the Beginning

Jesus ascended to heaven, but that wasn't the end. He left work to do. The Helper has come and put you on His team for sharing the Gospel. Don't just stand there! Jesus is coming back.

PENTECOST

The Spirit Comes

The disciples knew what was coming: they knew Jesus was leaving and that He would ascend to heaven. Still, they were afraid of being without their leader and teacher. In the days leading up to Pentecost, the disciples were afraid and anxious. They begged Jesus: "Lord, show us the Father, and it is enough for us" (John 14:8). They were fearful about where Jesus was going: "Lord, we do not know where You are going. How can we know the way?" (John 14:5).

To calm their fears and anxieties, Jesus promised the disciples that He would not leave them alone as if they were orphans (John 14:18), and He promised that He would send a helper—the Holy Spirit.

On Pentecost, Jesus made good on His promises to the disciples. On that day, they very clearly and publicly received the gift of the Holy Spirit. There was no doubt in anyone's mind: Jesus had made good on His promises, and the disciples were certainly not alone.

Fill in each blank with the correct word(s) from the following list:

understand	baptized	Jerusalem	tongues	Holy Spirit
fifty	grave	three thousand	languages	primary languages

Pentecost occurred _____ days after Christ's resurrection from the

_____ . People who spoke many different _____ from many different

countries had gathered in _____ . The gift of the _____ allowed

Jesus followers to speak in _____ . They spoke in _____ ,

which they had never learned. As a result, everyone was able to hear and _____ the

same message. This allowed _____ people to hear the Gospel, repent, and be

_____ .

REVIEW

tongues—

witness—

One Though Many

Language can be a massive barrier when trying to communicate with someone; trying to make sense of a foreign language is frustrating, if not impossible. To make things even worse, there are thousands of different languages spread out across the world, resulting in ample opportunities for communication breakdowns.

Communicating with one another was not always this frustrating. In Genesis 11, we are told there was a time when all people spoke the same language. Having only one language made communication so easy that the people worked together and plotted to build a tower to heaven! This gateway to heaven that the people tried to build is known as the tower of Babel. God saw the people's great pride in their arrogant plan to build the tower. So He confused their language, mixing up their speech and creating many new languages.

Notice how what happened at Pentecost is the exact opposite of what happened at the tower of Babel. At Babel, the world went from one language to many languages, and people could no longer understand one another; at Pentecost, people miraculously were all able to understand what was being said, despite the fact that they spoke many different languages. On this day after Christ's death and resurrection, creation was given a glimpse of what life was like before sin corrupted the world. Not only did Christ conquer sin and death on the cross, but He also restored life to the way it was before sin! Pentecost offered a glimpse of the restored language that God's people will enjoy when Christ returns.

On the arrow below, write the letters *a* through *f* to place the following events of human history in their correct order: (a) tower of Babel, many languages in the world; (b) the Last Day, when language will never again be a barrier; (c) God's creation has one language; (d) sin enters the world; (e) Christ's perfect life, death, and resurrection; (f) Pentecost, when language is no longer a barrier.

___ ___ ___ ___ ___ ___

Acts 8:26–40

PHILIP AND THE ETHIOPIAN

Did Not Our Hearts Burn within Us?

On the first Easter, the disciples walking to Emmaus asked themselves this question after they realized that their walking companion had been Jesus. Their hearts were burning with joy and wonder as Jesus taught them from Scripture. You have the same blessing as the Holy Spirit empowers your faith with Word and Sacrament. He sets a burning joy in your heart with the Good News of Jesus and leads you to share that joy with others.

The Source

The Holy Spirit brings you to faith, and His power is at work, keeping you in faith throughout your life. The Holy Spirit

a. calls us by the Gospel (He brings us to faith through the Means of Grace, Word and Sacrament.);

b. enlightens us with His gifts (He tends to our faith and lights our souls by bringing us the knowledge of God through the face of Jesus.);

c. sanctifies us (Working in the Word and Sacrament, through which He also calls us, the Holy Spirit gives us power for holy living and provides tools for good works.); and

d. keeps us in the one true faith (He faithfully preserves us in Jesus unto life everlasting.).

Write the letter of the statement of each working of the Spirit from the preceding list with the Bible verse below that best identifies or describes this work.

_____ And I am sure of this, that He who began a good work in you will bring it to completion at the day of Jesus Christ. (Philippians 1:6)

_____ To this He called you through our gospel, so that you may obtain the glory of our Lord Jesus Christ. (2 Thessalonians 2:14)

_____ For He who sanctifies and those who are sanctified all have one source. (Hebrews 2:11)

_____ For God, who said, "Let light shine out of darkness," has shone in our hearts to give the light of the knowledge of the glory of God in the face of Jesus Christ. (2 Corinthians 4:6)

How is the Holy Spirit at work in your life? How is His work important to you, both now and later in your life?

_____

_____

REVIEW

rejoice—

The Spirit at Work

Jesus came to save all people, regardless of nationality. The Holy Spirit gathers all lands and nations together in the Church. Acts 8:26–40 tells how the Holy Spirit sent Philip to a visitor from another country to explain the Word to him. Complete the following chart to tell how you see the Holy Spirit in His "gathering" function in the account of Philip and the Ethiopian.

The Holy Spirit Gathers	
Questions	
Events	
Attitudes	
Means of Grace	

Rejoicing on Our Way

Why do you think the Ethiopian's heart was burning within him as he and Philip parted company? What makes you think as you do? What do you think the Ethiopian did when he got home? Why is it important in your life that the Holy Spirit keeps your heart burning?

_____

_____

_____

_____

30

SAUL COMES TO FAITH

An Unlikely Choice

Read the account of Saul becoming a Christian. In the spaces provided on the timeline below, summarize the details in each set of designated verses.

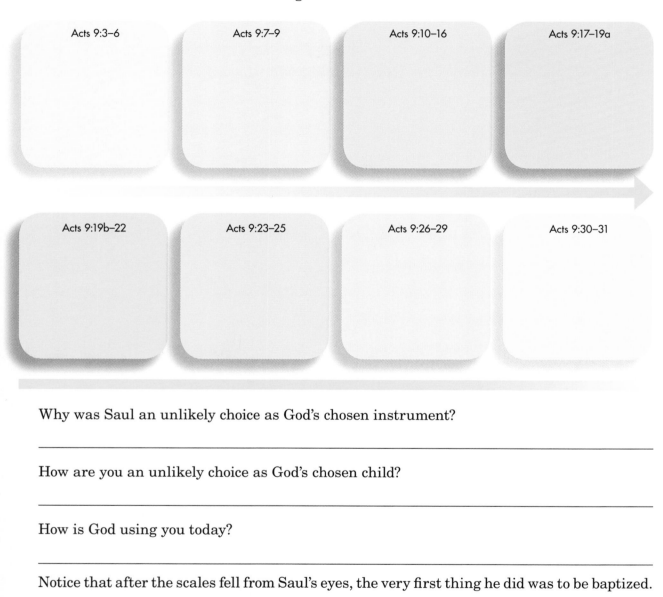

Acts 9:3–6

Acts 9:7–9

Acts 9:10–16

Acts 9:17–19a

Acts 9:19b–22

Acts 9:23–25

Acts 9:26–29

Acts 9:30–31

Why was Saul an unlikely choice as God's chosen instrument?

_____

How are you an unlikely choice as God's chosen child?

_____

How is God using you today?

_____

Notice that after the scales fell from Saul's eyes, the very first thing he did was to be baptized.

REVIEW

adoption—

conversion—

A Christian's Biography

Those who have come to faith have experienced a *conversion*, a changing from an old way of life—the natural condition into which we were born—to a new life in Christ Jesus. Draw lines to indicate whether each of the following statements describes the old way of life according to our natural human condition or the new life we have received by grace through faith in Jesus.

Old Way of Life

New Life in Christ Jesus

We are born in sin.

We gather with other Christians to support and encourage them.

We look forward to eternity in heaven.

We are enemies of God.

We are destined to eternal punishment for our sins.

We trust in the forgiveness Jesus earned for us.

We are baptized in the name of the triune God.

We talk to God in prayer.

We share the Good News of Jesus with others.

We anticipate receiving Christ's body and blood in the Sacrament for the forgiveness of sin.

We do not understand the things of God, and we rebel against them.

We forgive others as God in Christ has forgiven us.

We pray for ourselves and for others.

Newness of Life

Before Baptism, you wore the old self. Now, since Baptism, the new self has come forth because you are wearing Christ. Now, through the Holy Spirit, the new self produces good works. Even though Saul persecuted the Church, many "brothers" were kind to him. Can an enemy become a friend? Yes! By God's grace and with His power, amazing, unlikely things happen!

REMEMBER

If Christ is in you, although the body is dead because of sin, the Spirit is life because of righteousness.

Romans 8:10

GRADE 8 GLOSSARY

A

absolution—a remission (forgiveness) of sins

adoption—act or state of being received into a family as a child and heir

adoration—praising God for His qualities and His acts of grace and goodness

adultery—sexual relations between a married person and someone not his or her spouse; lust or any sexual act against God's will

agnostic—someone who argues we can't know whether or not God exists

alliance—a bond or union between individuals, groups, or states

alms—charitable donations; people who could not work lived off this; a lame man received the ability to walk instead of this

anoint—to apply oil in a sacred rite; to set aside for an office or sacred calling

apologist—someone who argues in defense of God or a person or cause

apostasy—the abandoning of previously held beliefs

ark of the covenant—special vault containing the Ten Commandments

ark—name for vessel in which Noah and his family as well as Moses were saved

Artemis—a Greek goddess; Ephesus was considered the central city for her worship

Asherah—Canaanite and Phoenician goddess associated with sexual love and fertility

atheist—someone who believes there is no God

authorities—those who have the right to tell us what to do and the responsibility to watch over us

B

Baal—Canaanite and Phoenician local idol, sometimes cast in the form of a bull

Baptism—application of water by God's command and combined with God's Word

betray—to disappoint the hope or expectations of; to be disloyal to

betrothal—a contract to marry, usually arranged by the families of the bride and groom

bind—to secure or tie up

birthright—double portion of the inheritance, leadership of the family, and the blessing to carry on the covenant promise

blasphemy—claiming to be God; or showing irreverence toward God

blessing—a gift from God

bullying—taunting or humiliating those who are weak

C

call (or "a calling")—summons; a vocation or an inclination

called—invited or summoned with a view to service

captivity—state of being confined or imprisoned

censer—an incense burner

cherubim—angels, especially in Old Testament, they appear with wings spread over the ark of the covenant

Christ—the Anointed One

Christian—literally, "little Christ," or someone belonging to or professing faith in Christ

circumcision—act performed on males; originally done to indicate identity as a follower of the true God

command—an order expected to be followed

commitment—dedication to a person or cause

Communion—another name for the Sacrament of the Altar; a joining or coming together

conception—the moment at which life begins

concubine—a woman to whom a man is legally bound in a form of marriage

confess—to acknowledge, reveal, or make known

confession—an acknowledgement of truth before God or others

confirmation—a rite designed to help a person identify with the life and mission of the Church; also an affirmation or verification

contrition—recognition of one's sin and the realization of one's inability to fix his or her brokenness

conversion—changing from one belief or perspective to another; a turning around

covenant—a binding promise or agreement

covet—a wrong and unhealthy desire to be, or to possess the things of, another

cursed—held under affliction

D

deliver—to rescue or set free

devoted—designated

disciple—a student who learns from a master or teacher; a follower of Jesus

divination—to foretell the future through omens, oracles, or supernatural powers

Divine Service—weekly service that includes the celebration of the Lord's Supper

E

entice—to coax or nudge away

entreaty—a plea or earnest request

ephod—an outer apronlike garment made of linen worn by Jewish priests in ancient times

eternal death—the unending separation from God of an unbelieving person's soul

evolution—theory that living things evolve from other living things

exile—a period of forced absence from one's country or home

exodus—a leaving or departing

exorcist—one who casts out demons

F

faith—trust or reliance upon God and His promises or upon a person or concept

faithful—steadfast; loyal; resolute to a person or cause

faithfulness—quality of remaining true to a commitment

famine—duration of time in which little or no food grows over a large area

festival—time of celebration or special observances; the Life of Christ portion of the Church Year

fisher of men—someone who knows Jesus' love and wants others to know it too

foreshadow—to prefigure or indicate beforehand

fornication—voluntary sexual relationship outside of marriage

funeral—an observance or religious service held when someone has died

G

genealogy—an account or list of one's ancestors

Gospel—the Good News that God sent Jesus to forgive and rescue us through His life, death, and resurrection

grace—to receive blessing not merited, earned, or deserved

guilt—feeling of responsibility for wrongs committed

H

heart—organ responsible for circulating blood through the body; true self; the part of us that only God knows

holy matrimony—marriage; the union of a man and woman as husband and wife

homage—an expression of high regard or respect

honor—to highly regard in thought, speech, and action

hosanna—a Hebrew word meaning "save us now"

humility—state of lowliness; opposite of being proud or haughty

hymn—congregational song of prayer or praise, usually in a stanza form

hymnody—the body of spiritual songs used in the Christian Church

I

idol—an object of devotion other than God

idolatry—practice of worshiping a false god

implore—to call or pray for earnestly

impudent—disrespectful, rude words

incarnation—the act of taking on flesh

inheritance—possessions passed down to recipients by those who have gone before them

iniquity—sin and wickedness

intercession—petition or prayer offered on behalf of another

J

jealous—unwilling to accept rivalry or unfaithfulness

Jews—those descended from Abraham through the line of Isaac and Jacob

judge—Old Testament deliverer; leader or official responsible for justice

justice—judgment involved in determining rights, rewards, and punishments

justification—righteousness that is ours in Christ Jesus; also, support for a position or condition

K

kinsman-redeemer—a close relative who avenged wrongful deaths, helped poor family members claim their inheritances, and married the widow of a dead male relative so she would be protected and cared for

knowledge—an intellectual grasp of the facts; an understanding of a particular subject

L

Law—God's decrees about how to live a holy life; it shows us our sin

leadership—effective guiding of others to achieve a goal

Levite—worker in the temple

liturgical—relating to an established procedure for worship

loose—to release or free (as in, to untie)

M

Magnificat—Latin for "magnify, praise"—the song of Mary

manna—bread miraculously provided by God for His people in the wilderness

marriage—a legally binding commitment uniting a man and woman

martyr—witness; one killed for his or her beliefs, including faith in Christ

Means of Grace—the Word (Gospel) and the Sacraments (Baptism and Lord's Supper)

meditate—think carefully about

mediums—persons claiming to be able to bridge communication between earthly and spiritual realms

mercy—not getting the punishment that is deserved; the feeling that motivates compassion

Messiah—the promised Savior

Midianites—a group of people who lived south and east of Canaan

missionary—a person who takes up the task of sharing the truth, often in foreign lands

N

natural selection—theory that states weaker species die out while stronger species evolve into stronger, more complex species

Nazirite—a person dedicated to God for life or for a period of time during which he or she refrained from wine, grapes, and raisins, never cut his or her hair, and avoided being around dead bodies—even when family members died; Nazirites were signs to all Israel that they were called to stand out as God's people, witnessing God's love to the nations around them

necromancers—those who conjure up spirits of the dead to foretell the future or do supernatural acts

neighbor—any and every person

nonfestival—time outside of the celebration period; the Life of the Church portion of the Church Year

O

obedience—act of fulfilling the will of another

obstacle—something that blocks your way or hinders your progress

old Adam—the corrupt and evil nature we inherit because of Adam's fall into sin

omen—occurrence used to predict or foretell future events

omer—a measure of about a quart or a liter

omnipotent—all powerful

only-begotten son—sole biological son

oppressing—an unfair use of power

outward appearance—what other people can see when they look at us and what they think about us based on what they see

P

parable—story used to make a spiritual point or to teach a spiritual truth

Passover—annual festival held in remembrance of God's deliverance in Egypt when the angel of death spared the firstborn of those whose houses were marked with the blood of a lamb

peace—a calmness and sense of being at rest

persecution—subjecting others to cruelty because of their beliefs or identity

Philistines—a group of people living in Canaan during the time of the judges and kings; enemies of God's people

pillar—an upright shaft or column

pilot—the captain of a ship; also, the act of steering a boat or ship

plunderers—enemies who steal, loot, or take possessions by force

prevail—to prove more powerful than opposing forces

Prince of Peace—one of Isaiah's names for Jesus

prophecy—a divinely inspired prediction, instruction, or exhortation

prophet—one who speaks messages from God; one who foretells future events

prototype—something or someone that provides a type or model for something or someone else

Purim—Jewish holiday celebrating the deliverance of God's people at the time of Esther

purity—set apart from immoral behavior; chastity

R

reassure—to remove doubts and fears

rebellion—to turn or act out against

rebellious—opposed to rules or authority

redemption—deliverance from sin; salvation

reform—to change and improve

regeneration—spiritual rebirth

rejoice—to be joyful

relent—to let up or back away from

remembrance—present manifestation of a past event or events

remnant—what is left when something else is removed

repentance—a change in direction; a gift of God that includes both sorrow for sin and a sincere desire to change

reproof—criticism for a fault (rebuke)

reprove—to scold or correct, usually gently or with kind intent

respect—to honor or hold in high regard

restoration—being brought back to a previous state, such as to a trust and belief in God

rite—a religious practice or ritual

S

Sabbath—day of rest

sacrament—a sacred act instituted by God that joins a visible element (or elements) with His Word and conveys the forgiveness of sins

sacrifice—to give up something of value for a cause

Sadducees—the highest Jewish leaders of their time

salvation—deliverance from sin and its effects

Samaritan—member of a group commonly looked down on by Jewish people

Sanhedrin—Jewish religious leaders led by the high priest; composed of rich, upper-class men

scheming—attempts to direct the course of events

Sheol—realm of the dead; place where God's judgment overtakes evildoers; a grave

signs/symbols—shapes or actions that represent people or concepts

sin—transgressions; iniquities; wrongs; evil; corruption

sinful nature—innate inclination to disobey God

slander—a malicious, false, and defamatory statement

sorcery—attempt to use power received from evil spirits or spiritual forces

spoil—items of value captured or otherwise taken from an enemy

sponsor—one who assumes responsibility for a person or cause

squandered—spent extravagantly or foolishly

steal—to take the property of another wrongfully

stiff-necked—stubborn; unwilling to listen

summon—to call someone to take a specific action

supplication—request made of God or another

T

tabernacle—the tent church built by Israelites, following God's commands, while living in the wilderness

temporal death—occurs at death when the soul leaves a person's body

tenacious—persistent; tending to hold fast; cling

testimony—authorization given of something as a fact

thanksgiving—expressing of gratitude to the giver for good things received

tongues—languages; also refers to tonguelike shapes, as in tongues of fire

transformed—changed in character or condition

tribulation—griefs, troubles, or sorrows

tribute—payment by one ruler of a nation to another as a sign of subjugation or price for protection

trust—reliance or expressed confidence; to rely upon or to place hope in

type of Christ—a biblical person or object having similarities to Christ and foreshadowing, foretelling, or pointing to the coming of Christ and His purpose

U

unconventional—unusual; eccentric

V

vessel—a container, such as a bottle, bowl, or cup, for holding something

victory—win

vocation—a calling from God setting a baptized person apart for His service; also, a job or profession

W

wisdom—good judgment; the ability to apply what one knows in everyday life and to make choices that lead to positive outcomes; to act in obedience to God and to express godly attributes in one's life

witness—to give an account of what has been seen, heard, and touched

worthy—qualified or acceptable

wrath—anger

Z

Zion—the hill in Jerusalem; another name for Jerusalem; also a synonym for God's reign and His people

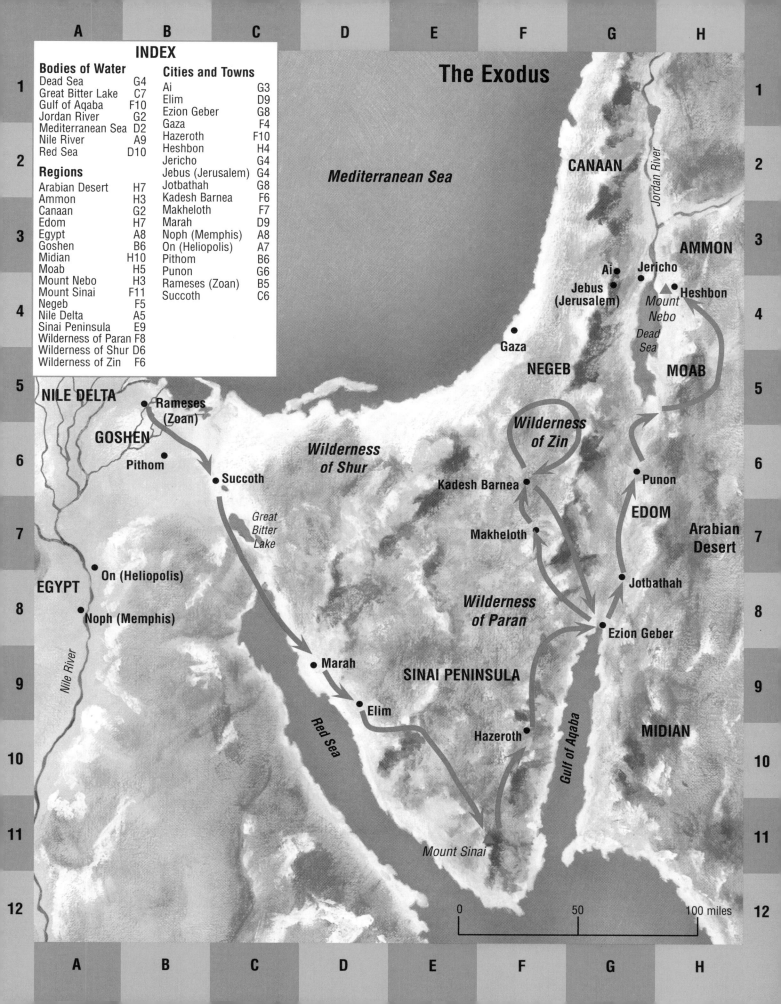

The Exodus

INDEX

Bodies of Water
Dead Sea	G4
Great Bitter Lake	C7
Gulf of Aqaba	F10
Jordan River	G2
Mediterranean Sea	D2
Nile River	A9
Red Sea	D10

Regions
Arabian Desert	H7
Ammon	H3
Canaan	G2
Edom	H7
Egypt	A8
Goshen	B6
Midian	H10
Moab	H5
Mount Nebo	H3
Mount Sinai	F11
Negeb	F5
Nile Delta	A5
Sinai Peninsula	E9
Wilderness of Paran	F8
Wilderness of Shur	D6
Wilderness of Zin	F6

Cities and Towns
Ai	G3
Elim	D9
Ezion Geber	G8
Gaza	F4
Hazeroth	F10
Heshbon	H4
Jericho	G4
Jebus (Jerusalem)	G4
Jotbathah	G8
Kadesh Barnea	F6
Makheloth	F7
Marah	D9
Noph (Memphis)	A8
On (Heliopolis)	A7
Pithom	B6
Punon	G6
Rameses (Zoan)	B5
Succoth	C6

Mediterranean Sea

CANAAN

Jordan River

AMMON

Ai · Jericho

Jebus (Jerusalem) · Heshbon

Mount Nebo

Dead Sea

MOAB

Gaza

NEGEB

Wilderness of Zin

NILE DELTA

Rameses (Zoan)

GOSHEN

Pithom

Succoth

Wilderness of Shur

Kadesh Barnea

Punon

Great Bitter Lake

Makheloth

EDOM

Arabian Desert

On (Heliopolis)

EGYPT

Noph (Memphis)

Wilderness of Paran

Jotbathah

Nile River

Marah

Ezion Geber

Elim

SINAI PENINSULA

Red Sea

Hazeroth

Gulf of Aqaba

MIDIAN

Mount Sinai

0   50   100 miles

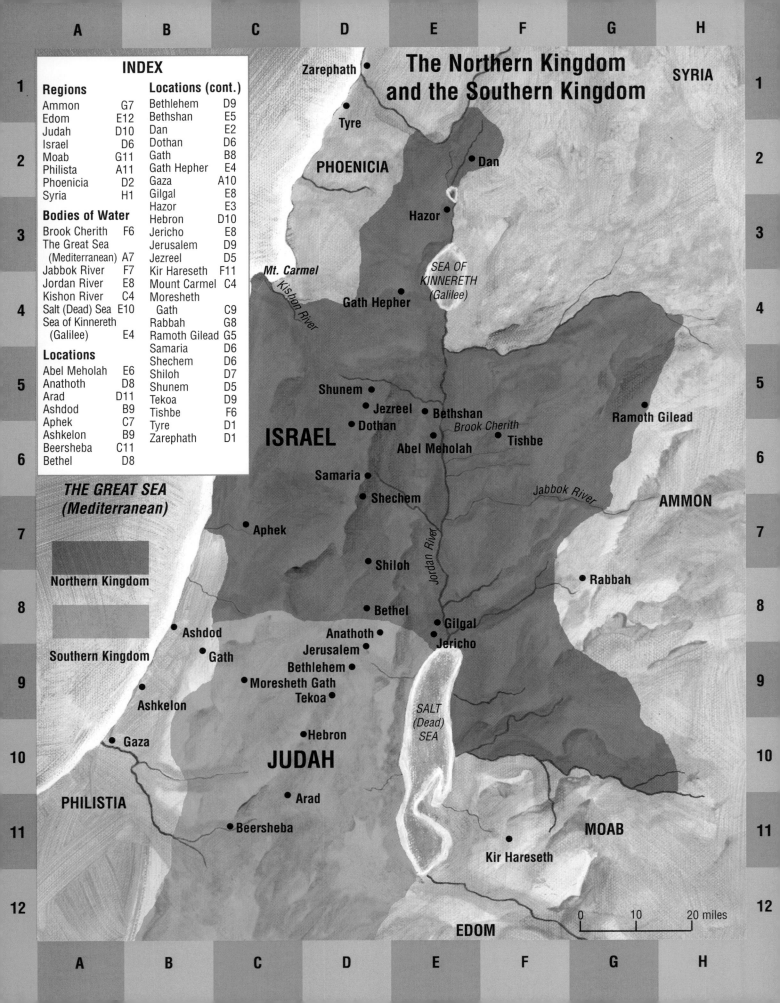

The Northern Kingdom and the Southern Kingdom

INDEX

Regions
Ammon	G7
Edom	E12
Judah	D10
Israel	D6
Moab	G11
Philista	A11
Phoenicia	D2
Syria	H1

Bodies of Water
Brook Cherith	F6
The Great Sea (Mediterranean)	A7
Jabbok River	F7
Jordan River	E8
Kishon River	C4
Salt (Dead) Sea	E10
Sea of Kinnereth (Galilee)	E4

Locations
Abel Meholah	E6
Anathoth	D8
Arad	D11
Ashdod	B9
Aphek	C7
Ashkelon	B9
Beersheba	C11
Bethel	D8

Locations (cont.)
Bethlehem	D9
Bethshan	E5
Dan	E2
Dothan	D6
Gath	B8
Gath Hepher	E4
Gaza	A10
Gilgal	E8
Hazor	E3
Hebron	D10
Jericho	E8
Jerusalem	D9
Jezreel	D5
Kir Hareseth	F11
Mount Carmel	C4
Moresheth Gath	C9
Rabbah	G8
Ramoth Gilead	G5
Samaria	D6
Shechem	D6
Shiloh	D7
Shunem	D5
Tekoa	D9
Tishbe	F6
Tyre	D1
Zarephath	D1

Northern Kingdom

Southern Kingdom

THE GREAT SEA (Mediterranean)

SYRIA

PHOENICIA

Zarephath

Tyre

Dan

Hazor

SEA OF KINNERETH (Galilee)

Mt. Carmel

Kishon River

Gath Hepher

ISRAEL

Shunem

Jezreel

Bethshan

Ramoth Gilead

Dothan

Brook Cherith

Abel Meholah

Tishbe

Samaria

Shechem

Jabbok River

AMMON

Aphek

Jordan River

Shiloh

Rabbah

Bethel

Gilgal

Jericho

Anathoth

Jerusalem

Ashdod

Gath

Bethlehem

Moresheth Gath

Tekoa

Ashkelon

SALT (Dead) SEA

Gaza

Hebron

JUDAH

PHILISTIA

Arad

Beersheba

MOAB

Kir Hareseth

EDOM

0   10   20 miles

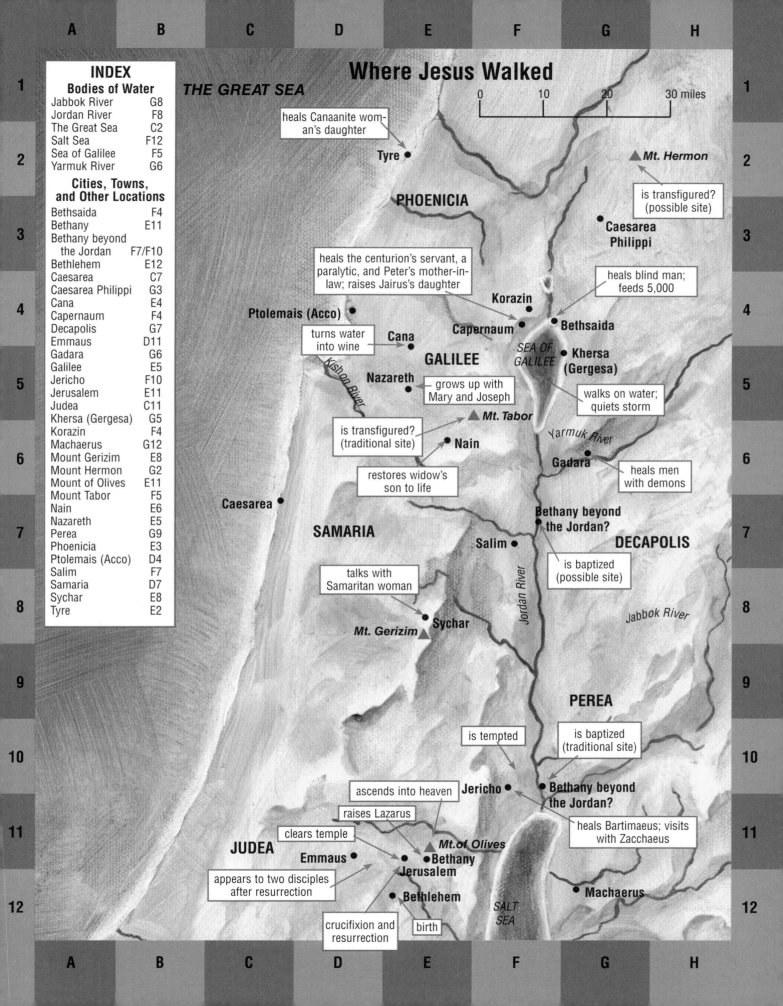

Where Jesus Walked

THE GREAT SEA

0   10   20   30 miles

heals Canaanite woman's daughter

Tyre

▲ Mt. Hermon

is transfigured? (possible site)

PHOENICIA

Caesarea Philippi

heals the centurion's servant, a paralytic, and Peter's mother-in-law; raises Jairus's daughter

Korazin

heals blind man; feeds 5,000

Ptolemais (Acco)

Capernaum

Bethsaida

turns water into wine

Cana

GALILEE

SEA OF GALILEE

Khersa (Gergesa)

Kishon River

Nazareth

grows up with Mary and Joseph

walks on water; quiets storm

is transfigured? (traditional site)

▲ Mt. Tabor

Nain

Yarmuk River

Gadara

heals men with demons

restores widow's son to life

Caesarea

Bethany beyond the Jordan?

SAMARIA

Salim

DECAPOLIS

is baptized (possible site)

Jabbok River

talks with Samaritan woman

Jordan River

Sychar

Mt. Gerizim ▲

PEREA

is tempted

is baptized (traditional site)

ascends into heaven

Jericho

Bethany beyond the Jordan?

raises Lazarus

heals Bartimaeus; visits with Zacchaeus

clears temple

JUDEA

▲ Mt. of Olives

Emmaus

Bethany

appears to two disciples after resurrection

Jerusalem

Bethlehem

Machaerus

SALT SEA

crucifixion and resurrection

birth

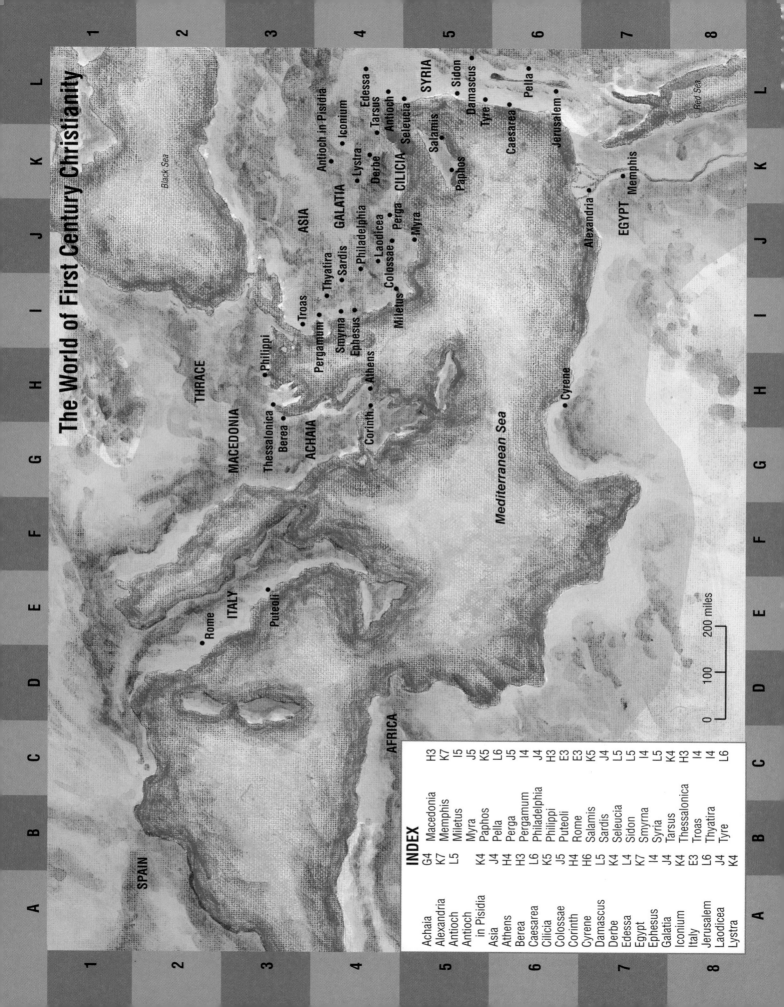

The World of First Century Christianity

SPAIN

ITALY
Rome
Puteoli

THRACE

MACEDONIA
Thessalonica
Berea
Philippi

ACHAIA
Corinth
Athens

Black Sea

ASIA
Troas
Pergamum
Thyatira
Smyrna
Sardis
Ephesus
Philadelphia
Laodicea
Colossae
Perga
Miletus
Myra

GALATIA
Antioch in Pisidia
Iconium
Lystra
Derbe

CILICIA
Tarsus
Seleucia
Salamis
Paphos

SYRIA
Edessa
Antioch
Sidon
Damascus
Tyre
Pella
Caesarea
Jerusalem

AFRICA
Cyrene

EGYPT
Alexandria
Memphis

Mediterranean Sea

Red Sea

0   100   200 miles

INDEX

Achaia	G4	Macedonia	H3
Alexandria	K7	Memphis	K7
Antioch	L5	Miletus	I5
Antioch		Myra	J5
in Pisidia	K4	Paphos	K5
Asia	J4	Pella	L6
Athens	H4	Perga	J5
Berea	H3	Pergamum	I4
Caesarea	L6	Philadelphia	J4
Cilicia	K5	Philippi	H3
Colossae	J5	Puteoli	E3
Corinth	H4	Rome	E3
Cyrene	H6	Salamis	K5
Damascus	L5	Sardis	J4
Derbe	K4	Seleucia	L5
Edessa	L4	Sidon	L5
Egypt	K7	Smyrna	I4
Ephesus	I4	Syria	L5
Galatia	J4	Tarsus	K4
Iconium	K4	Thessalonica	H3
Italy	E3	Troas	I4
Jerusalem	L6	Thyatira	J4
Laodicea	I4	Tyre	L6
Lystra	K4		